Livable Design

*From Commodity to Community
with Affordable, Adaptable, Beautiful
Home Design*

Jeffrey DeMure, AIA

Fountainhead Publishing
Granite Bay, California

Livable Design: From Commodity to Community with Affordable, Adaptable, Beautiful Home Design
Published by Fountainhead Publishing
Copyright © 2018 by Jeffrey DeMure, AIA
All rights reserved.

Fountainhead Publishing
5905 Granite Lake Drive, Suite 140
Granite Bay, California 95746
Email: fountainheadpublishing@jdaarch.com

Limit of Liability/Disclaimer of Warranty:

Editor: Chelsea Richardson
Publishing Manager: Sara Stratton
Cover Design & Chapter Illustrations: Hugh MacLeod, @Gapingvoid
Photos courtesy of Livable Design

Library of Congress Number: 2018940800

ISBN: 978-1-7322070-0-4 – paperback
ISBN: 978-1-7322070-1-1 – hardcover
ISBN: 978-1-7322070-2-8 – ebook

Ordering Information:
Quantity sales. Special discounts are available on quantity purchases by corporations, associations, and others. For details, contact the publisher at the address above.

Printed in United States of America.

GREG –   10/11/19

YOUR UNCOMPROMISING PASSION FOR
GETTING LIFE RIGHT, CHALLENGING
YOURSELF AND THOSE AROUND YOU FORTUNATE
ENOUGH TO CALL YOU FRIEND, COLLEAGUE
AND COMPATRIOT, IS AN INSPIRATION TO ME
BEST ALWAYS –

LIVABLE DESIGN

DEDICATION

I dedicate this book to the homebuilding industry.

To the people who take risks and love what they do.

To the people who do it all day in and day out, forgoing recognition and gratitude.

To the entrepreneurial American spirit that exists within homebuilding companies all over the country, and to the people all across this industry who have sacrificed, invested, loved, and agonized to make the American Dream a reality for millions.

CONTENTS

ACKNOWLEDGMENTS

This journey would not have been possible without the inspiring passion and loving support of so many people.

Thank you to the late Wes Justyn, the instigator who—with his trademark humor—lovingly challenged all of us in his sphere of influence to improve the world as we found it, to make the impossible possible. Wes, you were the inspiration behind Livable Design.

Thank you to Sheri Peifer, Todd Murch, and Erin Scherer for their tireless dedication and belief that the American Dream can impact so many more people in such a meaningful way. Your love for the future residents impacted by Livable Design continues to shine through.

I'm grateful to Shannan West, who helped get Livable Design off the ground, and Chelsea Richardson, who was an early adopter, organizer, and inspiration to continue the sometimes tedious but vital work of helping Jeffrey DeMure + Associates Architects Planners (JD+A) contribute to the creation of Livable Design with the Eskaton team.

Thank you to the team at JD+A for the unwavering encouragement and love they continue to show to their leaders, and for trusting that together, in unity, our future is bigger than our past—for ourselves and for millions of others.

Thank you to Katherine MacKenett for helping me to bring this book to fruition.

Finally, my eternal gratitude goes to my wife, Melanie, and our beautiful children, Emily, JT, Jeremy, and Brayden. You are a constant source of encouragement, love, and joy, fueling my greatest dreams for our family and our world, and instilling passion and purpose into my life.

To all of you and to others I may have neglected to mention here, thank you, from the bottom of my heart.

FOREWORD

An engaging narrative, Jeff invites us to take a journey. A journey that will impact our thinking and approach toward creating living environments that celebrate generations and support life's many experiences. With simplicity and candor within these stories, we can envision communities filled with Livable Design homes and connected spaces, bringing to life the vision cast by our dear friend, Wes Justyn, whose legacy is building beautiful, supportive homes for all. Through creativity, tenacity and the desire for transformation, this vision has given birth to hundreds and soon to be thousands of Livable Design homes for generations to come.

Sheri Peifer
Chief Strategy Officer
Eskaton

HOW I MET HUGH

I met Hugh MacLeod in 2013 when he spoke at The Vine conference in San Diego, California, and have been an admirer ever since. With his unassuming manner, Rapidograph pens, and Scottish brogue, Hugh is an enigma wrapped in an anomaly shrouded in mystery. Bright and early after a night of revelry, I spotted him in the corner of the conference with his digital sketchpad and wondered, 'Huh. I wonder how this is going to go?' Much to my surprise, at the conclusion of the program Hugh took the stage and proceeded to share his musings and sketches for each of the day's presentations, concisely summarizing the essence and feeling of each topic. Mic drop.

Fast forward to the writing of this book and I found myself pondering how best to sum up the significance and simplicity of Livable Design. On a whim, I sent the book to Hugh and asked if he'd be interested in illustrating it. You hold the result in your hands. Hugh read the book and encapsulated each chapter in a piece of art and I couldn't be happier with the collaboration. Each chapter begins with one of his pieces accompanied by his musings on the subject.

Should you find yourself struggling for how to best convey your message, your voice or your culture, reach out to Hugh at @gapingvoid and experience the magic for yourself.

INTRODUCTION

'INCLUSIVE' IS
A FACT,
NOT AN
IDEAL

@gapingvoid

To date, the home building industry is very good at getting people of the same demographic to live together. But getting people of different demographics to co-exist has been far more problematic, even with government "help."

And that's a shame. A strong community includes everybody. People of all different ages, class and, yes, all different levels of physical ability or mobility.

Simply put, Livable Design™ adds more thread to this tapestry and makes living with differences far easier and doable.

-Hugh MacLeod

Building Frustration

Perhaps you're a builder or developer. Or maybe you specialize in architecture or design. You've been in the industry for many years, and you've seen fluctuations in the market, as well as your fair share of successes and failures along the way.

Whether you're an integral part of a small company or a larger organization, you face an ongoing problem in the industry: the market continues to get more and more saturated with the things that used to be distinctive and unique to your company and your brand. If you're part of a larger organization, you may feel you're chasing an ever-shrinking share of that market. Or if you're part of a smaller firm, you're likely trying to break through this ceiling of distinctiveness—somehow.

Either way, you're having an increasingly difficult time getting your business to where you want it to be, from both a design and an impact perspective.

Complicating the situation, the best locations are more expensive than ever to build on. Land prices keep rising. As Will Rogers said, "Buy land. They ain't making any more of the stuff." And many municipalities make the entitlement and approval process incredibly convoluted.

"We have . . . a city [with] probably two or three hundred committees. Every committee is dealing with just one problem and has nothing to do with the other problems." - Alvar Aalto

Amid this backdrop, it seems impossible to stand out.

The frenetic nature of the homebuilding industry sometimes seems like being stuck on a hamster wheel—and it feels so limiting, so *frustrating*. No longer do you feel you're providing the American dream—a huge motivation for you when you started in this industry. Rather, your business has devolved to merely selling a product to consumers. You had bigger dreams, bigger goals than this. You wanted to impact more people in a more meaningful way.

To be certain, you also want to make more money. After all, the primary goal of any business is to stay in business and generate profit for the owners and shareholders. But perhaps just as important, you've always wanted to make an *impact*. You want the homes you design and build to help people and their families live happier, healthier, more complete lives.

You're exasperated by doing the same thing repeatedly and seeing the same disappointing results. You long to provide a means to distinguish yourself—not just now, but also in the emerging markets of the future.

But how do you break out of the mainstream mold and make a name for yourself and your company? And how can you do it without incurring undue risk?

You could build bigger homes, smaller homes, or ones with more creative floor plans. Chances are, though, that you've already been doing this consistently throughout your career. And so is everyone else. What once was distinctive is now commonplace. The bar for success is being defined by a market that continues to apply the same limiting metrics—and it's harder and harder to stand out amid the homogeneous sea of sameness.

Many of us have had enough of the "fad follows function" mentality of today's homebuilding industry! You're ready to get back to Louis Sullivan's concept of "form follows function." You need a new paradigm, a new mindset. You're ready to provide something that people really *want*, that would make their lives and those of their friends and families better. Something that will make the homes you build attractive to a wider cross-section of the homebuying population—not just now, but for many years to come.

But does this solution even exist?

Break the Mold

Yes, it does. And as my pastor, Don Roberts, says, "It's not that hard to be remarkable."

What if your next generation of designs aligned perfectly with your organization's ability to build them *and* included simple, inclusionary ideas to satisfy the ever-evolving population of a continually shifting market?

This solution is something my company and I have been working on for over a decade, and it's called Livable Design™.

This revolutionary new school of design focuses on providing living spaces geared toward comfort and adaptability for all stages of life—from a single, independent, and active lifestyle, to family life with children, to comfortably aging in place (or, as I prefer to say, *living* in place, because nobody wants to age, but everybody wants to live!). These new living spaces also mean that if you, a friend, or a family member ever experience mobility issues from age, injury, or disability, your home remains a welcoming space that allows you and your loved ones to continue to move and function, with comfort and dignity, within that space.

In any given market, at least 70 percent of builders are building for less than 35 percent of homebuyers, so it's no wonder there's so much commonality and similarity among offerings. That 35 percent represents the traditional family buyer, and that traditional family demographic shrinks every year. What Livable Design allows for is a broader penetration into something that has a deeper purpose and speaks the language of the people who are actually going to buy and *live* in these homes.

From a purely business standpoint, this expanded market share is the biggest advantage of Livable Design. But it's far from the only benefit.

Suddenly, you aren't just building houses anymore. You're building multigenerational communities designed to be genuinely *livable* and inclusive for a much greater percentage of the population.

You're making progress again. Not only is your business growing, but you're finally moving forward. What you're doing is significant—you're changing lives. And that sense of satisfaction and fulfillment brings joy back into your work and purpose to your life.

This is the promise of Livable Design. And I'm here to teach you how to bring it to life in your business. The intent of this book is to provide the *why* and point you to the resources that we've developed to provide the *how*.

A Passion for Inclusion

My name is Jeffrey DeMure, and I've been an architect for more than thirty-five years. I'm licensed in fifteen states, and I've put my architectural stamp on over one hundred thousand homes throughout the country. In 2005, I was the first architect to become president of the PCBC (Pacific Coast Builders Conference), one of the most significant and respected trade organizations and a part of the California Building Industry Association for homebuilders in the United States. I've also been a judge for numerous architectural design competitions across the country.

This professional experience has given me access to our country's best minds, ideas, and solutions for building: architects, builders, researchers, authors, and manufacturers.

I also lead Jeffrey DeMure + Associates Architects Planners, Inc. (JD+A), an architectural firm I founded in 2004 that now employs a team of thirty-five architects, land planners, artists, colorists, writers, an attorney and broker, and renaissance men and women. Half of our business consists of working with profit-making builders and developers that provide housing ranging from single-family detached to high-density attached. The other half provides solutions for older adults in the form of active adult, independent living, assisted living, and memory care communities. Our firm has received multiple awards, shaped new communities through our design standards, and actually gotten great amounts of our designs built.

I'm passionate about designing buildings that can work—projects that can be financed, approved, and built (the vast majority of everything we start actually gets built). I also have a passion for land planning, because if you take a home or a building and don't consider its context, then you're designing only part of the real solution. Integrating both land planning and architecture into new communities has taught me a lot about how people use their neighborhoods—both collectively and individually.

Beyond business, Livable Design was also borne out of real-life experiences—both my own and those of close friends and family members. In particular, I learned firsthand in my youth that the way our homes are typically built compounds the frustration and indignity of living with mobility issues. An estimated 24.1 million Americans live with a severe disability that interferes with their ability to perform one or more activities of daily living and/or requires the long-term use of assistive devices such as wheelchairs, crutches, canes, and walkers. Seven million of these Americans are children under fifteen years old. This is a staggering statistic, which only the homebuilding industry can impact on a mainstream basis, outside of egregious, bureaucratic or governmental control.

ONE IN FIVE AMERICAN ADULTS HAS A DISABILITY

-U.S. CENSUS BUREAU SURVEY OF INCOME AND PROGRAM PARTICIPATION JUNE-SEPTEMBER 2005 AND MAY-AUGUST 2010

When I was a twenty-two-year-old architecture student at the University of Arizona, a motorcycle accident left me with fifteen broken bones. My right arm, hip, ribs, and vertebrae were fractured. I had casts from my right biceps to my fingers and from my right hip to my ankle. For months afterwards, I was unable to walk unless I used bulky, specialized crutches.

When I was finally discharged from the hospital, my parents' home in upstate New York was the only place available for me to convalesce—so home I went. But I quickly learned that the home I grew up in, like most homes, wasn't built for someone with limited mobility.

For months, I was unable to bathe myself, access the bathroom, or perform other basic daily tasks without help. As a young adult, having my family members help me with those basic activities was mortifying, to say the least. While trying to navigate around indoor spaces that had never before seemed tight or constrained, I constantly banged my elbow, fingers, and my remaining good knee on door frames, walls, and counters. And getting up and down the stairs in that house on those crutches wasn't just challenging—it was downright dangerous.

These unexpected challenges added more stress, pain, and frustration to an already difficult physical and emotional recovery. After months of physical therapy, I healed. However, I never forgot how the loss of my mobility, independence, and dignity made me feel during this challenging time.

How to Get the Most Out of the Book

Livable Design is based on a simple, five-element approach to using inclusive features when designing and building homes. To be clear, it is not a substitute for the Americans with Disabilities Act (ADA) or other regulatory programs, and it shouldn't be construed as related. As I've said, this new strategy will not only win your organization greater market share, but also lead to a remarkably rewarding way of doing business that connects you like never before to the populations you serve. Within the pages of this book, you already hold the key to learning what you need to know to get started.

I suggest that you read through this book in its entirety the first time. Don't skip around. In the future, you may want to revisit some sections that describe implementation and the *why* to Livable Design—particularly if you're trying to explain the concept to someone else. I find that stories, rather than mere facts and figures, are always a more meaningful way to get one's point across, so feel free to share the stories in this book with others.

The idea of Livable Design may sound simplistic to your colleagues when you try to get them on board, in which case I suggest they read the book themselves. When it comes down to it, this mindset shift *is* remarkably simple. As one of my sons said when I explained Livable Design to him, "Duh, Dad. That's just common sense." And like Occam's razor teaches us, "the simplest solution is often the best one."

My Promise to You

You can be part of the Livable Design revolution, ensuring that this and future generations have access to attainable living environments that aren't limited by mobility. The great news is that Livable Design is easy. But it isn't something you can shoehorn into an existing design after the fact. You have to think about it, plan for it, integrate it, and—most importantly—design it.

Livable Design outlines the basic elements and principles you need to know so you can set out on this journey yourself—realistically, attainably, and profitably. I promise you: this new way of designing and building will change not only your life, but also the lives of the people you work with and build homes for. I know this because it has changed my life, those of my colleagues and our team at JD+A, and the lives of the people living in Livable Design homes that have already been built.

The gift you'll be giving to the communities you serve cannot be overstated. Once you begin incorporating the tenets of Livable Design into what you create, your business will flourish, and your credibility in the eyes of the public will rise exponentially.

My Goal

I dream of seeing one million Livable Design homes and multifamily units built over the next five years and, as a direct result, the transformation of communities and lives all over our great nation.

You can be a part of this dream, this mission. And you, too, can reap the rewards of being on its leading edge.

By working together to achieve this simple—yet challenging—goal, we can transform homebuilding and the lives of millions.

Let's get started.

Chapter 1

What Is Livable Design?

A HOUSE THAT
CHANGES AS
YOU CHANGE

@gapingvoid

It's a simple idea: Because we change over time, we should live in a house that can change with us—a house that can change as our needs change.

A house that has this idea baked-in to its very design, its very foundation.

-Hugh MacLeod

Welcome Home

Imagine you're one half of a young couple taking possession of your home for the first time. Your infant daughter, just six months old, fell asleep on the car ride over, and you effortlessly wheel her in the stroller across the seamless, zero-threshold entry without disturbing her. In an hour or two, she'll wake up, her curious, bright eyes taking in new surroundings that will soon become as familiar to her as your face. While she naps, you mingle with smiling friends and family who have come by to help you move in.

Your grandmother is there, too, tears of pride stinging her eyes as she navigates from room to room and orients herself to your new home. She's still recovering from her hip replacement surgery a short while ago, but she's up and moving independently, and the generous width of your new home's hallways easily accommodates her walker. After a peek into the bedrooms, she bustles into the kitchen to make lunch, scolding your aunt for getting the wrong kind of mustard. She heads for the built-in counter that's set just a little lower than the rest. It's just the right height for her to work while seated on the stool someone brings.

"You did well, kid," she says with a wink as you pass by with another armload of boxes.

You grin back, already picturing your daughter sitting next to her in that spot a few years down the road, pretending to chop vegetables and insisting she's big enough to help Great-Grammy make dinner.

Ample circulation space, multiple height work surfaces, and thoughtfully-placed appliances create a beautiful Livable Design kitchen.

You set down your boxes, hear a familiar bark of laughter out on the front walkway, and head in that direction. Your cousin Anthony has arrived, three pizza boxes and a six-pack of craft beer stacked carefully on his lap. Serving our country in the armed forces has left him without the use of his legs, but it hasn't dampened his irrepressible humor. His eyes widen in surprise as he wheels himself inside without a push over the typical threshold. He instinctively tucks in his elbows, always raw from wheeling around the wrong kinds of narrow spaces, but finds the wide entry allows plenty of clearance.

His posture relaxes as he navigates through the entryway, bathed in light from nearby windows, and he takes in a deep breath, releasing it in a long, low whistle as he looks around appreciatively. "Huh," he says. "This will work!"

Maybe an hour later, Anthony makes a trip to the bathroom and is allowed the dignity of using it without assistance—in and out of there with no trouble at all. He plugs in his iPhone in the family room and doesn't have to struggle to reach down low, because the plugs are higher up than usual, easily within reach. He sees your little nieces and nephews running around underfoot, flipping the lights on and off in the guest room, and he goes to investigate. Sure enough, the light switches are set lower along the walls, easily accessible to him and the kids.

You watch Anthony from the hallway as he lets this sink in: a house that easily takes everyone's age and mobility in stride without the look, feel, and *smell* of an institutional environment.

The moving truck is still parked out front, half full of everything you own, yet already everyone feels right at home. You do too, you realize, watching your loved ones move with ease from one space to another. This is a home you can be proud of, where you'll host parties and holiday celebrations for years to come. You can expand your capabilities as a host while eliminating the need to apologize for not being able to include everyone.

This is it. You're finally *home*.

Livable Design 101

The previous story illustrates the single defining characteristic of Livable Design: inclusivity. It embraces a much higher level of inclusion as to who is able to visit that home, live in it, grow old in it, and be part of that neighborhood for decades to come.

Those of us fortunate enough to currently live without mobility issues may not realize that, at some point in our lives, each of us is likely to experience this sort of challenge—and not only when we get older. Children, young people, athletes, wounded warriors—people of all ages and from all walks of life—can experience a temporary or permanent loss of mobility.

A Livable Design home creates an inclusive living environment that is affordable, adaptable, and beautiful. Its foundational design and construction allow for easy and inexpensive adaptability to changing mobility needs. The design incorporates all of these features practically and simply enough that builders can afford to build these kinds of homes, and more people can afford to buy them. Finally, a Livable Design home is beautiful instead of looking institutional—offering spaces that ease the heart and lift the spirit, instead of weighing you down and inflicting eye bruises with hospital-style finishes and appointments.

Imagine not having to worry about whether your own home will accommodate you if and when you find yourself in a limited-mobility situation due to an illness, injury, or advanced age. Envision not having to feel anxious or embarrassed when playing host for an evening or a weekend to someone who uses a walker, wheelchair, or cane, or even to a parent with young children in a stroller.

This is the magic and the promise of Livable Design. And it's yours to seize—for the betterment of your buyers, community, and business.

In this chapter, I'll provide an overview of some key aspects of Livable Design, including how it was originally conceived. I'll also provide a quick snapshot of what lies ahead in each chapter that follows, so you have a road map of where we're headed.

Origins of Livable Design

So how did we come up with Livable Design in the first place?

About twelve years ago, I was approached by the late, great Wes Justyn, who sat on the board of directors for Eskaton, a then-forty-year-old nonprofit aging services provider in Northern California.

Wes took me to lunch and said, "I've got this great opportunity for you guys. I want to build my ninety-year-old mother-in-law a cottage on our property near our home, where she can live close to us, but independently. I know there are things you can do in private homes, but I don't want it to look institutional. And what I've learned is that there are absolutely no resources available to me to do this." He shook his head in disbelief. "There has got to be a way for us to bring these basic accommodations to designers, builders, and the rest of the industry, so we can house people in a way that will allow them to age in place."

He made a great point, but I was skeptical. We started doing some research while the team at Eskaton did their own. They identified a study performed by AARP that said an incredible 90 percent of all people over the age of sixty-five want to live in their own home as long as possible.

Then we started looking at nationwide demographics. The silent generation (born mid-1920s to mid-1940s): 27 million. The baby boomers (born mid-1940s to roughly 1964): 76 million. That's 103 million Americans who are staying healthier and more active longer than any previous generation. What's more, this population represents such a huge cohort that it's a relief these older adults don't all want to move to senior-living communities! Organizations like Eskaton cannot build enough communities to accommodate them all.

Clearly, adequate housing that provides the adaptability, attainability, and beauty this population desires should be an absolute must-have for us as a society. And we need to be able to design homes that legitimately work for these adults.

Soon after this, a couple of the talented, insightful, and purpose-driven young leaders at my firm came to me and said, "We want to do this Livable Design initiative as a pro bono project for Eskaton, a nonprofit organization."

Now, I'll admit there were two things I didn't like about that sentence: pro bono and nonprofit. But then I started thinking about the benefits this design project could provide, the impact it might have. I also knew this kind of thinking had applicability way beyond older adults. What if we could be responsible for a completely new mindset in design and building, one that advanced inclusivity and accessibility to the forefront of building instead of embodying them as an ugly afterthought of ramps and stainless steel grab bars?

Now *that* was exciting. That was something I wanted our firm to be a part of.

Core Elements

To make a long story short, we spent the next eight years developing Livable Design, identifying what eventually became a short list of simple requirements that could not only be incorporated fairly inexpensively and easily, but also were available to every homebuilder across the nation.

And when I say simple, I mean it. We're talking about adjustments like hallway and door width to accommodate mobility-assistive devices and strategically placed blocking in the bathroom walls to allow for future support-bar installation.

Meanwhile, we've seen other industries start to incorporate this kind of thinking. Remember when glass ketchup bottles used to be skinny and upright so that the ketchup sat on the bottom of the bottle? Well, today the lid is wide, allowing you to set the bottle upside down in your refrigerator. The bottles are made of three-inch-wide, easy-to-squeeze plastic. Why? So it's easier to grasp the bottle and squeeze out the ketchup—no matter your age or ability.

We see inclusive thinking today in everything from kitchen utensils (OXO Good Grips) to plumbing fixtures (Kohler, Moen, and Delta's universal design product lines). These examples of universal design simply make sense, so they have made their way into mainstream culture. Inclusivity is all around us—*except* in how we build our homes. In this context, it seems shortsighted, right?

Now, if you have enough money to throw at the problem, you can custom build a perfect home that works for everyone. But we work with for-profit developers and builders, and at the end of the day, these are the people who supply the American dream. So here was our challenge: we needed to find the most valuable and cost-effective solutions that would create a user-friendly living space for people with mobility issues. And we needed these solutions to be affordable for all involved, from the builders of these houses to the people—from all socioeconomic profiles—who would buy them.

As I clarified earlier, I'm not talking about adherence to ADA requirements or anything remotely institutional or clinical. Rather, Livable Design is a seamless application of workable concepts that make life at home more respectful, easier, and safer for a much wider range of mobility profiles. In short, I've taken my years of experience as an architect and designer and my roles as a son, grandson, and father and woven all of this together into something that can *actually be done*.

What's more, meeting Livable Design standards can set your organization apart from the competition, giving homebuyers what they actually want and making a real difference in local communities.

When we started the Livable Design process, we identified 137 detailed standards that could be used to refine a typical home design. Over time, we pared that list down to the five most significant and impactful. These standards had to meet two key criteria: they (1) would allow someone with a mobility-limiting situation to stay in his or her own home, and (2) could not be difficult or expensive to include in the initial construction (but would be nearly impossible or very expensive to retrofit).

These five components came to make up the core elements of Livable Design. The rest are quality-of-life enhancements—nice to have, but not necessities. We'll get into the specifics of the five components in the following chapters, but first I want to address some common concerns that tend to come up when people hear about Livable Design for the first time.

Is This Really Worth It?

Here's the reality of our world: even if builders want to do something fresh, new, and exciting, they have the lenders and financial partners to deal with. Once, while showing one of my firm's clients an innovative, contemporary design (way before contemporary was popular), he told me that, even though he loved it, he couldn't build it. He explained why: "If I build something that is even a little bit different, and it doesn't perform well in the market, my lender will blame the failure on the design and on *me* for doing something different. If I build the same thing everyone else is building and the homes don't sell, they'll just blame the market."

What does this have to do with Livable Design? Everything.

Livable Design can be incorporated into any architectural style. It serves a virtually untapped market. And it is transparent. The risk profile is marginal. Plus, even mainstream lenders like a unique value proposition.

I understand the kind of fear-based thinking that our client expressed that day. It's not that difficult to relate to. Those of us who lived through the Great Recession get it. But if you honestly want to stand out and be successful in this highly competitive industry, you must manage your fears. You can't do what everyone else is doing, what you've been doing all along, and expect to see a marked difference in your results. Albert Einstein called this the definition of insanity.

This classic definition has been restated by Dan Sullivan, co-founder of the Strategic Coach, who tells his clients, "If you do what you've always done, you'll get what you always got." Status quo should not be your aim if you are seeking improved results. Instead, we have to be willing to try something different. Look, the safest place for a boat is to be anchored in the harbor, but that's not what it was made to do. That's not what *we* are made to do, either.

The trick is to take that first step on a foundation of *purpose*, and that is what Livable Design offers. This isn't just about designing homes that look good or have the newest appliances or the best color schemes. As an industry, we have done a masterful job of researching surface application to death, but we have done a lousy job of breaking through that surface to the substance—the foundation of design. Homebuyers can and will make these kinds of decorator changes every five to ten years anyway, as trends and tastes change, but structural changes are a different story.

If you can offer a home with the foundation and the fundamentals that will allow that home to be easily adaptable for each new stage of life, regardless of its owners' evolving mobility profile, your brand is going to stand out from the competition.

Back when we first figured out Livable Design, a third-generation legacy homebuilder asked our firm to design eight new models using the process. It was toward the end of the recession, and we were finally starting to see some green shoots of life in the homebuilding market after years of dormancy. After so many years of hard work to create the concept (and did I mention we did that work for free?), we were thrilled to get Livable Design out there and launch the next evolution of the homebuilding industry.

That builder was Harry Elliott III of Elliott Homes, and he was so inspired by our designs that he decided to call the homes "Innovations." He went on to build and sell over 150 Innovations homes and is still building them successfully today. I'm proud of Mr. Elliott's bold decision to build a community that will have long-term value.

Your Blueprint for What Lies Ahead

We created Livable Design with builders in mind. You need resources to give you the courage, capability, and confidence to build a new generation of homes purpose-designed *for* the people who live in them.

Yes, when you first try something different, you might be criticized. You may need to make a bit more of an investment in time, money, and focus. There will be a learning curve. You'll need guidance to set yourself on the right path. But in your hands and between your ears, you have everything you need.

I've organized the rest of this book to highlight the five key components of Livable Design:

Foundational. Foundational refers to the structural elements that go into a home to make it live and breathe Livable Design. You'll learn how to plan and allocate livable and functional spaces that allow for balance and flexibility for years to come.

Beauty. The last thing anyone wants is to come home every day to an eyesore of a living space, so we've made sure that Livable Design homes offer not only shelter, but also a sanctuary from the outside world Here's where you'll learn how to offer accessibility without sacrificing aesthetic.

Evergreen. Livable Design exponentially expands the cycle of ownership for a home, allowing for a space that can continue to adapt and accommodate changing needs over the course of an entire lifetime. I'll show you the steps needed to ensure that the homes you design work for homeowners at all stages of life—from young adulthood, to family life with children, and on into the homeowner's legacy years.

Community. Livable Design thinks beyond houses to the community they create by allowing older homeowners to stay in their homes and neighborhoods for years to come. Here we'll cover how this new paradigm shift in the building industry can lead to building a stronger social fabric through creating multigenerational communities.

The Home Sanctuary of the Future. Finally, we'll explore how Livable Design is already transforming the industry through the work my firm and clients are doing and how you can use it to transform your own business and the communities that matter most to you.

Livable Design means building better and smarter and with the belief that, as Dan Sullivan says, your future is bigger than your past. Once you see all that Livable Design offers you, your business, your reputation, and your community, you'll wonder why it took you this long to start incorporating such simple changes into the homes you build.

Everything begins with getting down to the nuts and bolts of this new concept. In the next chapter, we'll take a closer look at the foundational aspects of Livable Design.

Chapter 2

Foundational

GOOD DESIGN STARTS WITH NOT KNOWING EVERYTHING

@gapingvoid

Good design doesn't happen because the designer has all the answers. Good design happens because the designer starts off by asking A LOT of questions.

What are we designing, exactly? Who is it for? How much is it going to cost? What materials are we using? What are the technological limitations? How much time do we have?

After asking all these questions, then, and only then, does the designer put pen to paper.

Then God willing, an answer emerges.

-Hugh MacLeod

Life on the Edge

Our industry likes to think that the homes we create will function for the broad majority of the market, but that's far from accurate.

For instance, my ninety-one-year-old mother lives alone in a three-story townhome in central Connecticut. She's the quintessential Italian grandmother: highly independent, young at heart, and determined to spend her days visiting friends and shopping for fresh food—because good, home-cooked food with the people you love is the cornerstone of our culture.

On weekends when the weather is nice, she drives to the flea market to sell collectibles she finds at church fairs and estate sales. She uses the profits to help the homeless in her town—and then to play the quarter slots at the casino. She loves her home and is determined to stay there, even though her space wasn't built with someone with her mobility in mind.

The main culprit in her home? Stairs. They are *everywhere*.

Her bedroom is on the upper floor, and there's another set of stairs leading to the laundry room in the basement. That means she spends all day traipsing up and down the stairs—carrying loads of laundry, retrieving cleaning supplies, grabbing a quick change of clothes, you name it. And that's not all.

A detached garage sits a hundred feet from the house. And to get there? You guessed it—more stairs. Railroad-tie stairs. Railroad-tie stairs that get horrifically icy in the winter.

My poor mom is a heart attack waiting to happen—no, not her heart, but *mine* and my sisters!

For her, however, the daily battle with those stairs is unrelenting, and it has a huge impact on her life, as it has for the past thirty years. She's had not one, but two knee-replacement surgeries. She gets around fine, but the scary reality is that, like so many older Americans, she's just one slip and fall away from a total loss of independence.

The potential for my mom to fall is a constant source of anxiety for my sisters and me, because it doesn't have to be like this—not for my mother, and not for anyone else in her situation. If we would just apply to our home designs the same level of care and logic we use when we design a better can opener, we'd save ourselves an untold amount of pain, anxiety, and money.

Design That Works for Everyone

When people walk into a home that incorporates Livable Design for the first time, they look around a bit quizzically and say, "This house feels different. Why?"

They can't quite articulate it, because nothing about the accessibility built into the home jumps out and identifies its presence. It doesn't draw attention to itself or make the space feel clinical or institutional. It just blends quietly into the background, but you can *feel* the difference when you walk in.

It's open. There's more light. Instead of compartmentalized spaces that feel cramped, each area feels generous, even with smaller-square-footage floor plans. The walls are more like planes defining each space, allowing you to flow easily from one room to the next.

Because Livable Design elements work almost invisibly through each cycle of the owners' lives, people are free to simply enjoy these benefits and even take them for granted. Whether you're a two-year-old toddling around and tripping over thresholds, an older adult with a mobility-assistive device, or an avid skier with a broken leg, a home like this will work for you.

The foundational elements that make this possible aren't necessarily sexy or exciting, but they allow the space to sustain the entire life cycle of its residents for as long as they wish to remain living in their home. And if these foundational elements are not there? Then you might as well build the house's foundation on shifting sand, because it is extremely expensive and invasive to try and add them after the fact.

In my office, we call solutions that are not well conceived "duct-taped." That's how well today's homes function when you have a mobility issue. Plant-on ramps, institutional retrofit grab bars, and aftermarket toilet contraptions are not seamless, beautiful, or dignified. We can do better as an industry!

In this chapter, we'll go over the five foundational elements of Livable Design, including a detailed breakdown of where and how these elements function, so you can see how simple it is to incorporate Livable Design into a living space.

The Five Key Elements of Livable Design

As I mentioned before, when we first started working on Livable Design, we began with a list of 137 design elements and honed in on the most fundamental essentials. We landed on five cornerstone components that define the essence of Livable Design:

- A zero-threshold covered entry with a stepless approach and ample clearance
- A bedroom on the ground floor
- A fully adaptable bathroom on the ground floor with structurally reinforced walls
- A kitchen with ample clear space and multiple-height work surfaces
- Large doorways and ample circulation and clearance space

These five simple components can mean the difference between the stress of uprooting your life—starting over in a new home, a new neighborhood, or an older-adult facility—and the freedom to live in place in your own home as long as you desire. Let's take a closer look at each of these fundamentals.

The Entry

Your home is an extension of who you are. From the moment someone enters your home, you want that guest to feel welcomed, respected, and honored. For many people, that means not having to step *up* to the front door or entry.

That's why the first component of Livable Design is a stepless entry for at least one of the home's access points (front door, garage door, or other primary entry door).

This simple change is revolutionary in evolving the way residential space flows, and not just for those with mobility issues. When you're rushing out of the house in the morning on your way to work, your coffee hasn't quite kicked in yet, and you're not paying full attention, a four-to-six-inch curb can absolutely ruin your day—not to mention your really nice shoes.

A gentle slope leads to a wide entry door with a zero threshold.

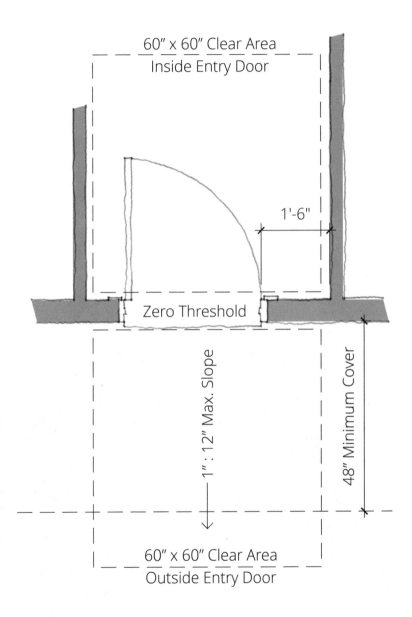

60" x 60" Clear Area
Inside Entry Door

1'-6"

Zero Threshold

1" : 12" Max. Slope

48" Minimum Cover

60" x 60" Clear Area
Outside Entry Door

It only takes a small distraction—grabbing your phone to read a text, corralling a rambunctious child, searching in your purse for your keys—and the next thing you know, you're in mid-air and falling.

From the front door to the interior spaces, following the flow from room to room, Livable Design means removing the steps.

Key components of the entry include a minimum forty-eight-inch-wide stepless walkway with a maximum 1:12 slope leading to a door protected by at least forty-eight inches of structural cover. There must be a five-by-five foot clearance space on both sides of the door, which has a zero threshold.

A walkway with a maximum 1:12 slope connects the driveway to the zero threshold front door.

The garage door often serves as the family entry, and a zero threshold is a simple — but revolutionary—way to elevate daily life.

Bedroom on the Ground Floor

The next component of Livable Design is having at least one bedroom on the ground floor in close proximity to the downstairs bathroom. This is key, because if you or someone else in your family have or develop mobility issues at some point, a bedroom on the ground floor can literally mean the difference between staying in that home or being evicted into a different living environment.

Being a gracious host is a cornerstone of our society. Having a home that can be inclusive for your aging relative, your friend who just returned from combat with a traumatic brain injury, or your niece who is in a wheelchair could mean the difference between you feeling the need to apologize for your home or feeling proud to own one that welcomes everyone.

FLEX HOME. *If a bedroom on the ground floor isn't possible given space constraints, Livable Design proposes an alternative: a flex home. In a flex home, stacking closets with a knock-out floor to install an elevator or wider stairs (at least forty-eight inches wide) to accommodate a chair lift can alleviate future mobility concerns. Either solution allows for a stepless transition between floor levels.*

Stacked storage closets are a great benefit in daily life and can be retrofitted to an elevator when needed.

Full Bathroom on the Ground Floor with Reinforced Walls

The third component of Livable Design is an adaptable bathroom on the ground floor. We never know when we will experience mobility issues or when we will host a guest who will require ground-floor accommodations for a weekend visit or an extended stay.

Small changes make a big impact. Strategically-placed blocking in the walls, added space beside the toilet, and a transfer tub work in harmony to create a beautiful Livable Design bathroom.

Much of what's done in residential design and construction is based on a "this is how we've always done it" mentality. We spent years digging beneath that stale approach to create better solutions. One such solution is a Livable Design bathroom, the key to which is adding eighteen inches to a typical hall bath, with the extra space located beside the pull side of the door.

This simple change ripples throughout the bathroom, making it possible to navigate using a mobility-assistive device. The shower is a minimum five-by-three-foot curbless shower (or has a removable curb); or the tub is a transfer tub, featuring a wide ledge to sit on while swinging your legs into the tub.

Reinforcing the walls costs very little, but a few extra half-sheets of four-by-eight-foot, three-quarter-inch plywood on the wall in a bathroom allows you to install fall-rated towel bars that don't pull out of the drywall when your kids swing on them or to add a support bar in the shower, if needed. Blocking in the walls is a cost-effective and highly efficient means of ensuring the long-term adaptability of a home. When planned for, this solution is simple, but as an afterthought it's mind-numbingly elaborate, difficult, invasive, and expensive to incorporate.

The implication is that the homeowner doesn't have to be concerned about where the structural member is behind the tile. You can put support bars and other features, for both utility and safety, wherever you desire: diagonally, vertically, horizontally—whatever works! This also means that while the home is new and under warranty, the builder (that's you) isn't getting calls to come replace the towel bar every time your tiniest customer does a pull-up at bath time and accidentally damages the wall.

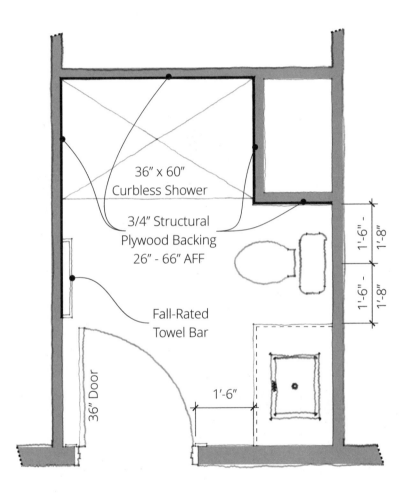

36" x 60"
Curbless Shower

3/4" Structural
Plywood Backing
26" - 66" AFF

Fall-Rated
Towel Bar

36" Door

1'-6"

1'-6" -
1'-8"

1'-6" -
1'-8"

1'-6" -
1'-8"

This curbless shower features non-slip mosaic tile, support bars that match the plumbing fixtures, and an adjustable wand shower head—all beautiful and all Livable Design.

THROW OUT THAT THROW RUG! *If a household item has the word "throw" in the description, the place to throw it is in the trash. Annually, an estimated 17,408 adults age sixty-five or older are treated in US emergency rooms for falls associated with rugs in the home. Even if a throw rug has rubber backing, people still trip over these in the dark. Rugs are, for many, an accident waiting to happen.*

A Kitchen with Ample Clearance Space and Multiple-Height Work Surfaces

The kitchen is the heart of the home, and when it isn't designed to be adaptable, it can, over time, become the barrier to being able to stay in your home in the long term. Most kitchens are not designed with adequate space to navigate with a mobility-assistive device. Livable Design provides a five-foot-diameter clearance in *U*-shaped kitchen configurations and forty-two inches minimum in other configurations. If an island is constraining the space, the floor must be finished under the island, and the island must be removable (think: dry island). You also need thirty-by-forty-eight inches of clear space in front of appliances. These simple dimensions make the difference between a kitchen that functions and a kitchen that forces you out of your home.

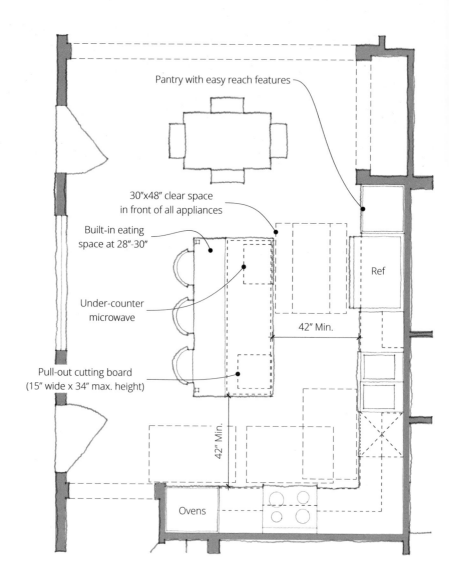

Pantry with easy reach features

30"x48" clear space
in front of all appliances

Built-in eating
space at 28"-30"

Under-counter
microwave

Pull-out cutting board
(15" wide x 34" max. height)

Ref

42" Min.

42" Min.

Ovens

The other key component here is having at least one surface (preferably more) that is no higher than thirty-four inches above the floor. An excellent solution for this is a multilevel island with a drop-down area. The lower level allows someone in a seated position to prepare food, and it's also ideal for a young child who wants to help. (A simple, old-school, slide-out cutting board also satisfies this provision.)

Multiple height work surfaces, with at least one no more than thirty-four inches above the floor, create an inclusive kitchen environment.

Large Doorways and Adequate Circulation and Clearance Space

Designers and architects are traditionally taught to think of circulation spaces as a necessary evil—a conveyance mechanism to get people from one space to another. Many of us were taught in architecture history class how Frank Lloyd Wright would purposely reduce halls and vestibules to minimum dimensions (very narrow, with seven-foot-high ceilings) so that the adjacent room would seem to "spatially explode" by comparison.

As a general rule, we encourage limiting circulation space as much as possible to allocate space into rooms instead of hallways. Livable Design takes it a step further by making any hallways a minimum of forty-two inches wide, with a preferred width of forty-eight inches.

A wide gallery leads to a stunning Livable Design kitchen.

The level of richness this simple change can bring also has incredible significance to those with mobility issues. Canes, walkers, wheelchairs, and strollers can easily move through such a space without banging up people's fingers or elbows, smacking into walls, or, in the case of a stroller, waking up a sleeping infant.

Incidentally, we don't even call these spaces hallways anymore on Livable Design plans. We call them galleries to shift the mindset away from pure utility and toward a more heightened experience.

Accommodating clearance space also means wider doorways. In a Livable Design home, all doorways are standardized to a width of three feet, with eighteen inches of space on the strike side of the door. This not only adds a unified, consistent aesthetic from one space to another, but also keeps purchasing simple for the builder by maintaining a uniform size for all doors and door frames. In a production environment, uniform sizes save time and reduce costs.

SPACE WHERE IT COUNTS. *We've all had the experience of walking into the tight space of a powder room and practically having to stand on the commode in order to close the door, or welcoming someone to your home and having to back into the entry hall to let them in. One drilldown element for Livable Design's enhanced circulation and clearance spaces is a recommended eighteen inches on the pull side of doors. This allows you to navigate any door in the home without having to contort into a yoga pose—something occupants of all ages and mobility profiles will notice and appreciate.*

A Foundation for Long-Term Prosperity

There's no good reason to continue to design and build 70 percent of new homes for a relatively small slice of the population. And even that small percentage is likely to get aged out of a home in roughly seven years as the family grows in size and matures in lifestyle. The average new homebuyer moves every six to nine years, many times because of lack of flexibility of the home.

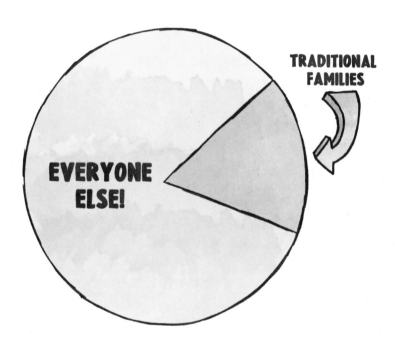

70 percent of all single-family detached homes are built for less than 35 percent of buyers.

That means these homes really weren't even designed for the demographic we think they were—not for that homeowner's actual lifespan, anyway. So who exactly are these homes designed for?

Think of it in terms of buying a car. Does the Mini Cooper you bought in your early twenties still work for you when you have children? You can make do for a while, but eventually it just doesn't fit your lifestyle, and you have to make a change. Wouldn't it be nice if this didn't hold true for your home, one of the biggest purchases of your life?

When you apply the basic components outlined in this chapter to new-home construction, you're creating a solution that is designed to work flexibly over multiple stages of the homeowners' lives. And this *shows*.

It shows when buyers walk in, and as they get a feel for the space, the air leaves their lungs (ahhh . . .).

These five core elements are the foundation upon which Livable Design is built, and they bring unparalleled respect, freedom, and dignity to the experience of living in these homes. That's a brand you can build the future of your business on—not to mention the future of entire communities.

Now that you have a solid grasp of the fundamentals, we'll look at how Livable Design incorporates aesthetics to create havens of warmth and comfort that are a joy to look at, live in—and continue to live in.

Chapter 3

Beauty

GOOD DESIGN
ISN'T JUST
TICKING OFF
ALL THE
DESIGN
BOXES ☑

@gapingvoid

It's too easy to think of design as just this "list," and all a designer has to do is go down the list, ticking off all the boxes until the job is complete.

It doesn't work that way. It starts off with a blank piece of paper, which is another way of saying, "An infinite set of possibilities."

And then that infinite set is made finite, honed by the limitations and compromises of time, money, technology, talent, client needs, and the laws of physics.

It's an organic process and it's beautiful and powerful to watch coming together.

But it doesn't "just happen."

-Hugh MacLeod

A Stark Comparison

In my business travels, I find I'm often checking into my hotel late at night after the other guests have already arrived and received their room assignments. In other words, I sometimes get whatever is left over. And more often than not, what's left is one of the ADA suites.

I've stayed in enough of these ADA "suites" to be able to say that an ADA room at a three-star hotel is like something out of a bad *B* horror movie. Bars and hoses are everywhere; equipment and devices hang from the walls. Yes, these rooms will accommodate a wheelchair or a walker, but it's as though the people who designed the rooms ticked off every box on a checklist of the bare minimum technical requirements mandated by law, without any thought to the experience of an actual person, disabled or otherwise, staying in the space.

Everything about these rooms screams "institutional." Even the shower curtains are ugly, chosen entirely to satisfy a basic requirement.

Compare this, though, to the experience of an ADA suite at a higher-end hotel, like the Ritz-Carlton or the Four Seasons. When you walk into one of these ADA suites, it's like walking into your own private spa.

For instance, if you get up during the night or in the morning when it's still dark, walking into the bathroom triggers a soft, glowing light that illuminates your way. The glow comes from a strip of motion-activated LED lights just bright enough to show you what you need to see without slapping you fully awake.

The light is not the only thoughtful touch. Support bars blend in to the decor with a nice oil-rubbed bronze finish that matches the plumbing fixtures. The roll-in shower features a stylish tile with a beautiful linear drain. Each little adaptation like this makes you feel nurtured and loved, like a little hug from the space itself.

That's a pretty massive difference from feeling like you're starring as the feature creature of the week in the two-star ADA room.

The chief executive officer of Eskaton, Todd Murch, went on a tour of these kinds of hotel rooms—the good, the bad, and the ugly—when they were doing their research for Livable Design. It was then that we all started to realize the work we needed to do to create the space where Livable Design can exist.

At the end of the day, we wanted to focus on creating inclusive spaces geared toward hospitality. Our homes wouldn't offer merely shelter; they would offer *sanctuary*.

That's the essence of Livable Design.

A Beautiful, Welcoming Home

The best hosts go to great lengths to make you feel comfortable in their homes. This is the role of beauty in Livable Design. We've defined what beauty means in everyday life, finding fixtures that not only are pleasing to the eye, but also accommodate a wide variety of mobility profiles. These seemingly opposing purposes are simultaneously addressed to create a hospitable environment instead of a hostile one.

Since we want to design and build homes that offer inclusivity without sacrificing elegance and joy, the concept of beauty in Livable Design focuses on taking the "hospital" out of "hospitality." The last thing anyone wants in a living space is for it to feel clinical or institutional. Rather, we want it to be warm, inviting, and comforting, honoring and respectful to every person who crosses our threshold, making each guest feel loved and cared for.

The incorporation of beauty is a key element of this ambition. As an architect, I like to say, "A thing of beauty is a joy forever, but ugly just hurts every day."

When you live in a place full of unresolved elements (ADA!), what you end up with, day in and day out, are eye bruises. And there's no reason why people should have to settle for this simply because of a mobility issue—not when perfectly workable solutions that are cost effective for everyone involved can be seamlessly, beautifully integrated into the space.

In this chapter, we'll take a closer look at defining what beauty means in Livable Design, as well as the key components to include to set the stage for a finished space that's adaptable, attainable, *and* beautiful.

Beauty, Defined by Livable Design

On the surface, within the context of Livable Design, beauty has the same components you'll find in any great design: structure, function, and delight (An update of 1st century BC architect Vitruvius, who called it commodity, firmness, and delight.)

Livable Design creates beautiful, modern, supportive spaces.

In Livable Design, however, the key element of beauty that we're striving for is *elegant simplicity.* You'll find this in the organization of the spaces and in the location of windows, doorways, and planes that define those spaces. For example, one of the key elements of Livable Design is wider hallways. However, since circulation space already takes up a great deal of area in a home, minimizing circulation space as much as possible can lessen the feeling of wasted space. Think of the home as a detached loft rather than a series of compartments. This is beautiful, elegant, simple.

Everyone wants to live in a place that looks good— that's just how we're wired. And living in a space that a person considers beautiful has a huge impact on his or her happiness and well-being. I recall a former team member who participated in a lottery system for the "privilege" of buying a home. The market was hot, and she and her husband felt desperate. When their names were called, they were handed a lot number and a home plan. When I went to congratulate my young colleague on her new home, I found her *crying*.

She didn't get the house or location she wanted, and she was miserable. I don't know about you, but I didn't get into this profession to make people miserable. A person's living space absolutely impacts his or her happiness.

Each little piece built into a home is one part of the whole, and to arrive at a beautiful, whole space, each piece needs to work together in harmony in terms of size, color, material, texture, and more. This means that being able to find and source fixtures and hardware that are both Livable Design-compliant and aesthetically pleasing is of paramount importance to the success of this concept.

Fortunately, we've spent the last ten years refining this process to be straightforward while providing for creative expression. Our firm has spent untold hours in countless meetings with a variety of professionals from multiple fields to integrate the best of all three considerations—inclusivity, cost-effectiveness, and beauty—into the selections of recommended design parameters, hardware, and fixtures.

Our selections are affordable and easy to incorporate; they work together to create a design that can be built on budget and on time. We've taken into consideration usual and customary processes inherent to wood-frame construction. From handsome (and fall-rated) support bars and bathroom-tissue dispensers that match the plumbing fixtures to curbless showers that extend the floor, we've identified the best of the best for the next generation of inclusive homes.

LIVABLE DESIGN–COMPLIANT FIXTURES AND HARDWARE. *Curious about what Livable Design-compliant fixtures look like? Visit the website at livabledesign.com for a complete list of the Livable Design Core and Builder's Choice elements, as well as case studies and a virtual tour of a Livable Design home.*

The reality is that you can't do everything. Livable Design–compliant does not equal ADA-compliant, and it's not "ADA Lite" either. It's about giving a sense of joy, respect, dignity, well-being, and peace to each space. To that end, what we can do is to put considerable thought into each component selected for a space. Together, these add up to a beautiful, adaptable, attainable, and unified expression that never ceases to amaze the homeowner, regardless of his or her stage of life.

Beauty on the Inside

To be clear, Livable Design is by no means intended as a "paint–by-numbers" solution. Think of it more as a set of well-conceived guidelines to be incorporated by an architect or designer who will then apply discretion, wisdom, and experience to add proportion, balance, unity, and harmony to the organization of living spaces.

Livable Design provides the context and framework to achieve great results. If your goal were to build an ugly eyesore, you'd have to work a lot harder to do so within these parameters.

As mentioned previously, you'll find a complete list of our recommended design features, hardware, and fixtures at the Livable Design website. But some of the key components are

- Curbless showers
- Fall-rated support bars, towel bars, and bathroom-tissue holders that match the plumbing fixtures
- Easy-to-use lever-style plumbing fixtures and door handles
- Circulation spaces with a minimum width of forty-two-inches
- Zero-threshold entries

- Three-foot-wide doors throughout

- Multiple-height work surfaces in the kitchen, with at least one at a maximum height of thirty-four inches

- Ample lower drawer storage in the kitchen

- Electrical outlets 20″ above the floor, light switches 42″ to 48″ above the floor

The accessibility of a zero-threshold entry is clear enough, but you might wonder how it adds beauty to a home. When you can extend a plane within a building so that your eye keeps moving as you experience the home, you increase the flow of that space. When nothing is there to stop the eye, it perceives this as being more visually pleasing than a limited space, and it makes the space feel bigger, more gracious, and more beautiful.

The same is true when you walk from a living space out onto a patio. The first thing the eye registers is that the space simply continues, from the interior of the home to its exterior. Classically trained architects have been doing this since the outset of modern architecture—creating spaces that flow from inside to out.

You might also be wondering about the beauty of three-foot-wide doors. From a design standpoint, the beauty here is that it brings unity. When you look around a space and see a two-foot-wide door, a two-foot-six-inch-wide door, and a two-foot-eight-inch-wide door, all in the same room or area, your subconscious will register discomfort. When you use too many parts and pieces, it's unsettling, like having three different hairstyles on your head at the same time. It's just plain disconcerting. Eliminating the mélange of door sizes contributes to a unified, beautiful expression.

These templates aren't intended to limit creativity. On the contrary, they are the beginning of creativity. In teaching Livable Design to as many professionals in this industry as we can, our objective is to make sure people realize they don't have to go out and reinvent the wheel—and every architect knows that a solution is richer when it has constraints. This program is a building block for homes that can remain attainable, adaptable, and beautiful for generations to come.

The Rewards of Beauty

When you experience a space that integrates beauty through structure, function, and delight, you can't help but feel it uplift your spirits. It speaks directly to your heart. This is the greatest joy an architect can have: to watch people experience a space they've designed and see joy on their faces and hear excitement in their voices.

That's ultimately what Livable Design seeks to do. In creating inclusive living spaces, we seek to spark joy in the lives of those who will live, work, and play in these homes.

And that joy reflects on you, the builder. It reinforces your credibility, your business, your value system, and your bottom line. At its core, Livable Design is a purpose platform. It improves people's lives through improving how they experience their space. And it helps restore a sense of meaning and purpose to what we do.

In starting to incorporate the tenets of Livable Design into what you build, you do have to break a few conventions. But, as they say, to make an omelet, you have to break a few eggs. This isn't just something new; it's something that functions better for a much larger percentage of the population. After all, nearly one-third of all American families have at least one member of the family with a disability.

You can build houses so beautiful, adaptable, and flexible that people will want to live in them their entire lives. In the process, you can reap the benefits of being on the forefront of this revolutionary process of designing and building homes.

In the next chapter, we'll take a closer look at how Livable Design homes adapt to each new stage of their owners' lives.

Chapter 4

Evergreen

WE GROW
AS
YOU GROW

@gapingvoid

What people think they want in a home is shelter, comfort, and convenience in a new, trouble- free, warranty-rich wrapper. But we strive to offer so much more than that.

We strive to create a community that expands the typical demographic slice and combines all of these parts and pieces into a sanctuary. A whole being, so much greater than the sum of the parts.

Let us state it plainly and proudly: This is real. This is not some idealized, academic utopia of the future; this is real people living in the real world, here and now, and luvin' it.

-Hugh MacLeod

Lessons from Grammy

I come from a big Italian family, and my grandmother lived with us for a good part of every year. So when I was a kid, she was a huge part of my life. We were close—so close, in fact, that when I was in elementary school, I used to literally run home from school every day to have lunch with her. I'd get home, out of breath, and we'd eat whatever she'd made and watch soap operas (don't judge). Then I'd run back to school: rain, snow, or shine. (Keep in mind, this was in upstate New York with four serious seasons.)

No matter what life had in store for me on any given day, Grammy was always there to offer her support, kindness, advice, and love. The daughter of Italian immigrant parents and one of thirteen children, she raised five children of her own without a husband during the Depression (he died of pneumonia when their youngest was less than a year old).

Me and my beloved Grammy in 1969.

And she was without a doubt one of the classiest women I've ever met—incredibly bright, well read, a great sense of humor, just an absolute joy to know. I may not remember everything she ever told me, but I'll never forget how she made me feel: loved.

My parents owned and operated a bakery, which kept them abundantly busy, so Grammy was often the one to keep the home fires burning. She was always the first person up in the morning, cooking meals and helping around the house. She made holidays special by fixing traditional Italian dishes: smelts for Christmas and sausage bread for Easter. Her love and care made our lives special.

But when Grammy was sixty-three, I watched this wonderful, vibrant woman suffer a debilitating injury that absolutely destroyed her quality of life.

She broke her hip in a car accident, an injury that initially put her in a wheelchair and, later, a walker. Before my eyes, she went from being one of the most independent, lively individuals I'd ever known to needing to be taken care of every day just to perform her basic activities of daily living.

She couldn't get in the front door by herself, because someone had to carry her walker up the steps to the entry. Ugly pieces of supportive apparatus began to appear all over the house, including the bathroom, because the height of the water closet no longer accommodated her. And even with those assistive devices to help, there still wasn't room for her to negotiate her walker around the sink to comfortably reach the water closet.

For a woman with such an independent spirit, this was humiliating. But it didn't end there.

She was exiled from her favorite space in the house: the kitchen. The counter space, sink, and stove weren't made for someone navigating a wheelchair, using a walker, or needing to sit down in order to wash and chop vegetables, stir pots, and perform all the other tasks associated with cooking the foods she loved to make.

The environment she lived in was hurting her. It no longer allowed her to be the person she truly was.

Back then, there wasn't much I could do about this. I watched her deteriorate to the point that, within fifteen years after the accident, she had to move to a nursing home. She had no cognitive issues, but over time, her body just stopped working. I think that this was because her environment kept her from doing the things that gave her purpose and identity. Her time at this "convalescent home" was a death sentence. She lived there until the time of her death at age ninety-six.

Forty years later, when a couple of young professionals in my organization came to me and said, "We want to do this Livable Design program as a pro bono effort," I remembered Grammy. And I knew we were about to embark on something that could make a tremendous positive impact on countless lives.

A Home That Honors Us All

To embrace Livable Design is to honor and respect the need for human dignity and to acknowledge the reality that most of us, at one time or another, will experience mobility issues.

Nobody wants to age; we all just want to live. But a consequence of living is getting older, and the vast majority of us want to continue to live comfortably in our own homes for as long as possible. The industry calls this "aging in place," but what Livable Design really allows is *living* in place through generations.

Since our mobility needs change over the course of our lifetime, our homes need to be capable of changing with us. Retrofitting a home *not* initially built to accommodate these changing needs can cost anywhere from $50,000 to $250,000—an incredible expense, and not one many families can bear. And even with this investment to make changes, the results are far from seamless. Ultimately, at the point that our homes cannot be adapted to us, we are left with no choice but to leave.

The evergreen nature of Livable Design, however, with features like its wide galleries and doors and blocking in the walls, means the structural pieces needed for the home to adapt to its occupants are already in place. That home can adapt to the variety of life cycles the residents will go through over the course of owning and living in that home.

In this chapter, we'll define what it means to have an evergreen design, exploring how the features and conveniences of these homes help us to live happier, healthier, and safer lives throughout the entire life cycle of a family's time in the home.

What Is Evergreen?

Thanks to advances in technology and healthier lifestyles, many Americans are living longer and continuing to lead active lives well into their later years. As I mentioned previously, AARP conducted a study of older adults in which 90 percent of those surveyed reported a desire to stay in their own homes and communities as long as possible.

Even the best-designed custom home simply won't accommodate this desire at certain points. But Livable Design was created to extend this time period in a way that's actually attainable for everyone involved.

However, the evergreen nature of Livable Design doesn't just benefit us in our legacy years. It provides both us and our guests with adaptability for how we want and need to live at all stages in our lives. In other words, "evergreen" means taking a flexible and evolving approach to the livability and visitability of our homes.

When I was in my early twenties and broke more than a dozen bones in my body, I learned firsthand that mobility issues—whether permanent or temporary—can strike at any time in our lives. And many of the same adaptable features and fixtures that aid older adults with mobility issues are just as helpful to parents of young children.

For instance, one little touch we include as part of Livable Design is something simple: a detachable-wand showerhead in every shower. If you've ever wrestled a giggling three-year-old into having his or her hair washed, you can attest to how incredibly useful such a device is.

A zero threshold shower feels spa-like and allows people with mobility issues the ability to bathe with independence and dignity

Or take another adaptive feature we recommend: the bath shelf, something institutionally referred to as a transfer tub, which we've reimagined to be beautiful as well as functional. This is essentially a ten-to-twelve-inch extension that enlarges the outer edge of the bathtub. When you're young and single, you can use this to sit and give your dog or cat a bath, or to rest a cup of tea while you soak in the tub with a good book. Once you have children, you have a place to sit while you bathe *them*. And when you hit the empty nester phase and you're getting older, having this simple tool to ease your transition into and out of the tub is an incredible benefit.

A wide ledge at the edge of the tub offers a spot to put your book, sit while entering the tub, or easily bathe children.

At all stages of your life, this simple touch adds amazing value and high-level function. We've learned to live without these features, but it's the kind of thing you never knew you needed until you have it (like the universal design ketchup bottle). And once people experience these added conveniences and assistive features, they're going to wonder how they ever got along without them.

The added space in this gallery and kitchen feels modern and welcoming and will allow its residents to circulate easily, even with a mobility assistive device.

Even the pantry door is 36" wide—all spaces promote easy access with Livable Design.

Millennials buying homes today might swear they never plan to have children, but being able to easily move a couch or carry their surfboard into the living room to wax it while they watch Netflix—thanks to the generous clearance of the doors and hallways—is something they'll absolutely appreciate. Then, before they know it, they settle down and *do* start having children. And friends and family members of all ages and mobility profiles can visit for short or long periods of time without being negatively impacted, thanks to the Livable Design features of the home.

The bottom line is that the evergreen nature of these homes gives them much broader appeal. Through flexibility and thoughtful consideration of the legacy a home can support, Livable Design can adjust to the needs of you and your family, whatever the composition of that family may be.

So when that millennial homebuyer starts having children and realizes the need for a larger home after all, that family's Livable Design house will go on the market—where it will be snapped up by an older couple, perhaps empty nesters looking to downsize and needing a home that will accommodate their future needs. The life cycle of a Livable Design home is so much more dynamic and inclusive than a typical home. And the resale value is incredible!

Evergreen for All Life's Seasons

As we've discussed, the evergreen nature of Livable Design

works for homeowners at all stages of their lives. Let's take a closer look at each one of these stages.

Active Younger Adult

Let's say you're a single buyer purchasing your first home. The house's wide doorways and hallways accommodate a revolving door of roommates moving in and out, along with that kayak you decided to buy on a whim. You can enjoy nights of revelry with friends and come home with less likelihood of a trip-and-fall injury, thanks to zero-threshold entries.

Rough day at work? That shelf in the bathtub is perfect for a glass of wine or a mug of hot tea while you soak your stress away. You can even set your book or a device there to watch the game.

And that horrible couch your roommate brought?

A zero threshold entry and wide front door make moving day significantly easier.

The one that, in any other house, would stay *with* the house, because it is so hard to maneuver through tight hallways and around corners? That goes with the roommate once your new spouse moves in, because it's as easy to carry out as it was to carry in.

Married with Children

Soon after your new spouse moves in, a soft-close toilet seat becomes a must: it's spring-loaded, so when you give it a little push, it goes down by itself. Yes, a toilet seat that puts itself down with barely a nudge. Bam! Your relationship is saved.

A year or two later comes baby number one. The detachable-wand showerhead and bath shelf work together to create an effortless (sort of!) bath time—one where Mom and Dad don't have to deal with a kid who screams like he or she is being tortured. Wider doorways and zero-threshold entries mean you can transition your sleeping child from the stroller to inside the home without jarring the little one awake. And raised electrical plugs mean you don't have to put the baby down or get down on one knee to charge your smartphone.

Then along comes baby number two. As the children grow, they're able to function in their own living space as independent, small humans. The lower light switches mean the kids can reach them, and lever handles instead of knobs on everything from the doors to the sink taps are easier for little hands to use. (You can even turn those lever handles with an elbow if your hands are full!) Pulls instead of traditional knobs for drawers make them easier to open as well.

Multiple-height countertops in the kitchen give the children room to help with dinner or sit and do homework, remaining a part of the family dynamic. There's even a cutting board only thirty inches above the floor, just their height for that age when they start saying, "I want to help!"

The unintended consequence of lowering the microwave from its usual spot above the stove? Independence!

Fast forward a few years. Those pull-ups the children inevitably do on the bathroom towel bars? No problem. The bars are fall-rated for an adult, so they're not going anywhere. And if someone breaks a bone? Well, it's not fun for anyone, but in a home designed to keep you moving and functioning, regardless of your current mobility profile, you can still get around and take care of yourself and feel respected and honored in your own home, instead of feeling like a burden.

Your home's accessibility features also mean that Grandma can come for a three-week visit over the holidays. You can really enjoy your time with her, because she can function just as effortlessly and independently here with her cane or walker as she does in her own home.

Club Sandwich Generation

Matriarchs and patriarchs of the silent generation and first wave of baby boomers are living longer, and the phenomenon of the boomerang child born during the 1980s and 1990s has emerged. (The boomerang child is the one you throw out and keeps coming back.) What has transpired is a baby boomer couple simultaneously taking care of their parent(s) *and* their adult children. This phenomenon has evolved to the point where 37 percent of people under thirty are living with a parent. In many cases, these boomers are "caring for" their Generation X or millennial child (who often moves in with a child of their own) as well as the boomer's own eighty- or ninety-something parent. This has effectively created the "club sandwich" phenomenon of the reluctantly responsible boomer couple.

Enter multigenerational living. Today's families demand a different type of home—beyond what the core of the homebuilding market currently produces. Some extended families live together out of necessity, and some out of cultural mores. When Livable Design is incorporated into the new-age home, these living arrangements are possible and even comfortable. It is no longer a compromise to have multiple generations living under one roof. What I've found in my career is this: when you can present an idea with just a few simple truths about it, and it's designed with what's important to people, its value increases exponentially in the consumer's perception.

In 2011, when the Great Recession could still be felt, we worked with a national homebuilder client to bring multigenerational living to Northern California and Northern Nevada. This homebuilder was able to tap into an unmet need, effectively offering "a home within a home," as they call it. The features were not available on every home plan offered, nor at every homesite. It was, however, a great solution that created a significant distinction amid a bland landscape of ubiquity.

To their credit, that same homebuilder has expanded into the active-adult market and has made the investment to incorporate Livable Design components into the fourteen models we designed, ranging from 1,200 to over 3,000 square feet. We included two multigenerational models for a caretaker or family member to live in.

Their reward for this modest, yet earnest, investment? Eighteen months of being the top-selling community in their fairly large market of 145 new-home communities in a greater metropolitan area of about 1.8 million people.

Active Older Adult, Empty Nest

As I recounted previously, older adults are one fall away from losing their independence and being stuck in a skilled nursing facility to rehabilitate. But a Livable Design home's zero-threshold entries, ground-floor bedroom and bathroom, curbless shower, and support-bar-friendly walls all result in a considerably lower risk for this type of injury than for someone in a traditionally built house.

If you do suffer a loss of mobility or other health issues, the zero-threshold entries can easily accommodate a walker, a wheelchair, or a rolling oxygen tank. The bathrooms are eighteen inches wider, likewise made to accommodate mobility-assistive devices. And even if you don't need any of these things, you will almost certainly have friends and family members who do. Your home is a sanctuary of safety, comfort, and dignity and a well-balanced aesthetic for yourself and these loved ones.

Features like the bath shelf and detachable shower wand in the bathroom and the removable toe-kicks and lower work surfaces in the kitchen make it possible to sit as you complete everyday tasks: bathing, meal preparation, dishwashing. This is vital if you can't stand for long periods—or at all. In Livable Design–compliant kitchen cabinets, the highest shelves pull down, so the items you need are reachable without a trip-hazard stepping stool. All of these built-in features are beautiful to look at, highly functional, and remarkably cost-effective when the alternative is considered.

We can see how at all stages of life—from childhood to young and middle-adulthood, and all the way to our older years—a Livable Design home offers incredible evergreen adaptability. The value of such a home is undeniable, and once buyers understand what you're offering them, they can't help but respond to it—or to how walking across a zero-threshold entry through the open spaces of these beautiful homes makes them feel. A bonus for you is that they become unpaid spokespeople for your company.

In the next chapter, we'll take a closer look at the final piece of the Livable Design equation: the way these homes work together to create stronger, more vibrant communities.

Chapter 5

Community

LIFe BeGINS WITH ReD BeNCHeS

@gapingvoid

When you celebrate an everyday object, you elevate its significance and it becomes a cornerstone.

Once you've got this in place, it adds a unique heartbeat and personality to the neighborhood, giving the neighborhood a common point of interest. Giving it a there there, if you will.

-Hugh MacLeod

A Missed Opportunity

I grew up in a small town in upstate New York. A single man named Mr. Woolfred and two sisters (not his) lived next door to us. (I'll never understand how he landed that living arrangement in a small town in upstate New York in the 1960s!)

Mr. Woolfred was a train conductor and, in my eyes, the coolest guy I'd ever met. He lost the use of one of his hands due to an injury, but he never let that slow him down. He raced midget cars and shot guns. He even gave me my first one-hundred-miles-per-hour experience in his 1964 Buick Riviera (with a 450 horsepower wildcat engine!) and my first shotgun at age eleven. (Things were a lot different back then.)

In essence, Mr. Woolfred was like my cool adopted uncle, and he was an integral part of my development. Living in a multigenerational neighborhood gave me the chance to have this experience. I bet you, too, can remember an older person who had a strong, positive influence on you as a child.

Passing down knowledge, wisdom, and stories from the older generation to the younger is such a fundamental aspect of society, and yet it has largely been lost. Many blame our culture of busyness, but I think the cause is more deeply rooted.

Our communities are designed to be homogenous places composed of people who are demographically similar. If we continue to design these places that are ubiquitous, homogeneous, and shrink-wrapped, we're going to continue raising children who miss out on the opportunity to connect with an older generation, and our older generations will miss out on the chance to mentor our youth—something the elderly yearn for.

Build Communities That Last

Over the life cycle of any community, homes will change hands. People move out and move on, and new people come in. Interestingly enough, less than 13 percent of age-qualified homebuyers want to live in an age-restricted community (meaning age fifty-five and older). They'd much rather stay in their own homes and neighborhoods, remaining a vibrant part of the community they've established over the years.

The reality for most of these people is that their current home can only take them so far, unless they're in a position to do one of those expensive retrofits we talked about in the last chapter. And even then, you can't exactly widen your hallways to accommodate a walker or a wheelchair.

However, these older adults *can* move into newly built Livable Design homes within their existing communities. Such homes would allow residents to remain a part of the same neighborhood and maintain their existing social customs: shopping at familiar stores and participating in the same churches, clubs, organizations, and groups they've been a part of much of their lives. This allows older people to *live* in place—still in their own home rather than an independent or assisted living environment or an age-restricted community.

Because Livable Design creates more inclusive communities where people of all ages and all walks of life can live together—and do it attainably—it democratizes residential design. Livable Design incorporates solutions appropriate for people of all ages and mobility profiles.

Suddenly, gone are the age-restricted ghettos or those homogenous communities intended only for people between the ages of thirty-five and fifty-two, with their 2.5 children and 1.2 days. And in the place of these communities, we'll see neighborhoods where growing families live next door to septuagenarians and octogenarians who've been stalwarts in the community for generations. These older adults bring years of wisdom, sensitivity, and perceptiveness for life's ups and downs to their communities, helping weave the social fabric that connects us all.

And our communities will be stronger for it.

In this chapter, we'll take a closer look at how Livable Design leads to stronger, more inclusive communities and all the benefits that come with this.

The Heart of Any Community

To date, the homebuilding industry has done a masterful job of designing communities where socioeconomically aligned residents coexist in an environment tailored to that specific demographic. While government agencies have attempted to legislate socioeconomic diversity and include a more expansive cross-section of society, these efforts have a ways to go.

But a healthy community is a rich fabric that's woven together by a variety of people from all walks of life—people of different ages and, yes, different levels of physical ability or mobility. And this is something that's not easy to find in a community today.

Simply put, Livable Design adds more thread to this fabric.

The reality is that what gets built is what builders and developers understand. And to understand things that happen outside of your own life experiences is a difficult and sometimes scary endeavor—especially when the success of your business is on the line. This goes back to the story I shared earlier about the lender blaming the builder versus the market's assessment of how far outside of "typical" a project is. Once we really understand the concept of Livable Design, we will be able to explain it with confidence and excitement, and those we share it with will understand its simplicity and impact, giving *them* confidence in turn.

In essence, we can do a better job than we have been doing. One significant and often overlooked way to do this is to create communities built to foster generational diversity. We should be able to have the experience of walking down a street in our own neighborhood and hearing the laughter of a baby and an octogenarian, side by side. As designers, developers, and builders, we have the capacity to raise awareness of the possibilities in the communities we build. Our hands shape the evolution of our neighborhoods and communities.

At some point, you have to ask yourself if you are designing and building the kinds of homes that will not only appeal to more buyers, but will strengthen communities all over this country.

If the answer is no, it's time to rethink what you're building.

Your Friends and Neighbors

What's so important about Livable Design is it adds another component to the type of inclusivity needed to build a stronger social fabric. And it does this by acknowledging and honoring that some people have physical disabilities, regardless of their age. My family and I have friends of all ages with various mobility challenges—from older adults, to people my age who've experienced the amputation of a limb, to friends with disabled children.

In order to appreciate what Livable Design has to offer in terms of broadening the housing market, it's important to know the facts about the disabled population in this country. An estimated fifty million Americans have a disability. That's nearly one in five Americans, affecting roughly a third of all families.

The idea that this many people may not be able to live in a home that accommodates their needs or get around the com- -munity isn't just sad—it's a loss to us all.

The number one goal of Livable Design is to accommodate people who have been excluded from typical mainstream housing. And this goal does nothing if not lend itself to building a stronger community that is more representative of the families who actually live and work there.

It doesn't take a ten-thousand-square-foot lot with a large, rambling single-story home to make Livable Design work. It just takes a few well-thought-out ideas to be incorporated in the right way. Some of these are Livable Design, and some are just good community planning. But at the heart of this

IF THEY DON'T INCLUDE COMMUNITY EVENTUALLY, THEY'RE NOT REAL VALUES

@gapingvoid

lies facilitating multigenerational living and making it easier for people who have mobility issues to be able to get around and do more easily the things they need to do.

The amazing thing about the homebuilding industry is that we're one of the last industries to be disrupted. Look at recent changes to industries like technology, automotive, and manufacturing. Each has experienced major innovations that have disrupted the industry norm and established a new benchmark. Livable Design offers a comprehensive way of thinking about and providing solutions for housing for all people. Yes, it challenges some existing design norms along the way, but when the rewards are so monumentally high, it's clear that it's time to embrace this change.

The Eight Elements of Community

Before we ever developed Livable Design, our firm identified and began to incorporate Eight Elements of Community into each of our new communities, and Livable Design communities are no exception. We believe every community needs to embody each of the following principles in order to be enhanced to fulfill its ultimate potential.

The Red Bench

When I was in Italy with my family some years ago, I had opportunities to wander the streets early in the morning. I noticed how the tiniest of spaces were designed to be special.

A little niche, no larger than a phone booth turned on its side, would contain a bench and a few colorful pots, and suddenly it became a destination.

Thus, The Red Bench became a symbol for this concept. It's an inexpensive community-building component that creates a meeting space and gives a community a little character. A professor of mine used to say, "Paint it red, and call it a feature." In my experience, when you celebrate an everyday object, you elevate its significance, and it becomes a cornerstone.

Our firm's signature element of this kind is to put an actual red bench in a strategic location in communities we've designed. Once you've got this bench in place, it adds a unique

The Red Bench is more than an idea—we have designed and fabricated real Red Benches for unique projects we've designed, such as The Life Center in Orangevale, California.

heartbeat and personality to the neighborhood, giving the neighborhood a common point of interest.

The Third Place

We have work, we have home, and then we have a third place—where we gather and socialize, take the pulse of the neighborhood, or just take a deep breath and *be*. For many communities these days, this place is a coffee shop. It can also be your church, a pub, or a library. Ray Oldenburg's wonderful book *The Great Good Place* identifies this phenomenon as part of the cultural and social fabric we yearn for. Starbucks has built an empire around this principle.

MAKe THE THIRD PLACe COMe ALIVe

@gapingvoid

Connectivity

In this context, connectivity refers to a permeability between the residential and commercial districts of a neighborhood. Whether that's decorative paving, enhanced landscaping, or a gateway portal that creates a threshold experience from the homes to where the shops begin, this design aspect provides a little keyhole punch between the different nodes that make up a neighborhood. That directs foot traffic from the residential area to the commercial one, creating a more unified expression for the community.

Walkability

A community's walkability is defined by the experience you have while on the journey and incorporates such qualities as interesting scenery and destinations: an orange tree that blossoms once a year and smells amazing, a gazebo in the park overlooking a fragrant rose garden, or a row of quaint shops with interesting displays in the windows. Walkability also means you can walk comfortably, safely, and smoothly from one place to another.

Placemaking

Places are defined through identity and familiarity. When a name catches on and becomes a common part of the community's lexicon, a place is made.

Every piece of land has a story. Placemaking is about telling people that story and sharing it with the community so the people who live there understand, and can retell, the history. When people find significance in a cultural, physical, or historical item of interest—something that either still exists or is still relevant—and celebrate it, placemaking occurs. Maybe that means including a stand with a placard to show where a species of butterfly migrates through this spot every summer.

A tip: *do not* name a place after the amenity you destroyed to create it. For example, don't name a development Babbling Brook Estates when there's no longer a babbling brook and the estates are townhomes. The key to placemaking is authenticity and extrapolating the real story of the land on which you're building.

Wayfinding

Wayfinding refers to the network of signage and cues for how you get from one place to another. Street signs are the most basic form of wayfinding, but communities have many opportunities to evolve and enhance a simple walk beyond the fundamental. Neighborhood markers or icons, thematic public art, a network of uniquely designed benches, street furniture, lighting, landscape material that changes by district—the possibilities are endless for how you can invite people to experience a journey through the community.

Meaningful Open Space

There's open space, and then there's *meaningful* open space. Just because you have a park does not mean you have meaningful open space. Meaningful open space is imagination space. It's space that isn't programmed within an inch of its life. From an impromptu puppet show, to craft fairs or a weekly farmers' market, to a space for an annual community Christmas tree lighting, this space offers flexibility for people to gather and celebrate, visit, and support local culture and commerce. The scale isn't as important as the right proportions and design.

My favorite example is an overlooked, oversized median space in Sacramento, California where three streets come together. The neighbors got together and landscaped the median, adding a fountain, a bench, and a drinking fountain. Keyhole Park is now the comma in the sentence of a walk across two streets. Everyone stops for a few minutes on the bench or just to take a deep breath before continuing.

How well the open space is embraced by the community is one of the indicators for what elevates open space to the status of *meaningful*. And the spirit that's represented by this little jewel box of a civic space has made it unique within the neighborhood.

Cultural Infrastructure

Cultural infrastructure is the connective tissue that holds a community together. It is the threads that reach out of the new community and weave into the fabric of the existing community. This includes destinations and community services such as retail, restaurants, churches, schools, and offices. In essence, cultural infrastructure takes a mere subdivision and turns it into a community.

The Real Value of Community

Livable Design is extraordinary all on its own, but when you combine it with the eight elements of community described above, they work to expand each other, adding incredible inclusiveness and richness to the experience of living, working, playing, or visiting any given neighborhood. All of a sudden, you have kids growing up with other kids who are different from them. Some of these kids may have different levels of physical ability, but they are treated with the dignity and respect due to all people by the very environment they're living in.

This kind of community, by its nature, discourages bullying, discrimination, and intolerance. That means those kids—all of them—grow up to be better citizens. And there's no higher purpose for a community than this.

Community isn't something you necessarily need in order to physically survive. However, it's what ultimately helps make life worthwhile—to have people around you who reflect your shared humanity, a shared appreciation for culture and heritage, and respect for other's values. So much of life could be improved by civil discourse. As a friend of mine says, "The beginning of understanding comes through the conversation." Community allows for the conversation to take place.

I've seen a lot of hokey trends pop up in architecture and planning over the last twenty years. My desire to add something meaningful and substantive to the narrative is what ultimately led me to Livable Design.

When you distill the essence of the human experience down to its core, you arrive at a single question: What do people need to be happy? While we're each ultimately responsible for our own happiness, an environment that is beautiful, attainable, and adaptable to our needs creates a space for happiness to flourish.

Every community has a soul. It's up to us—those who design, plan, and build these communities—to ensure that spirit is one of joy and inclusion. Think ahead to thirty or so years from now, when you'll look back over the course of your career. What is it you would like to be known for? What is your legacy?

Chances are, it's the hope that you've left a lasting, positive footprint in the world through your work.

I can't think of a more powerful way for those of us in this industry to do that than to incorporate Livable Design into the next generation of homes built in this country.

Now that you've seen the real power of Livable Design to create stronger, more inclusive communities, you're poised on the threshold of a new beginning—for you, your business, and your community. In the next and final chapter, we'll look at what's just ahead over the next horizon, and how Livable Design has the potential to reshape what we think is possible.

Chapter 6

The Home Sanctuary of the Future

"GREEN" IS NOT AN ASPIRATION, BUT A BASELINE

@gapingvoid

Sustainability should be about more than just "green." Human sustainability—being able to live well in your own home as long as you want—is a higher calling of sustainability.

That Livable Design is sustainable goes without saying. It's part of the DNA.

If we want A FUTURE, then we have to make Livable Design THE FUTURE. It's that simple.

-Hugh MacLeod

Livable Design in Action

It was a warm summer day, with a bright blue sky. More than one thousand people were in attendance as we celebrated the grand opening of our premiere Livable Design community: The Cannery in Davis, California.

The Cannery in Davis, California, is the first 100% Livable Design community.

California's first farm-to-table new-home community, the Cannery features 547 homes nestled on 100 acres with a 7.4-acre working farm, parks, bike trails, shops, and restaurants. The homes provide a variety of lifestyle options in a range of densities. At the high end of the density spectrum, there are thirty dwelling units per acre four-story stacked flats and eighteen dwelling units per acre three-story townhomes. In the medium-density range, there are small-lot detached homes in four configurations: homes clustered around common pedestrian courts, alley-accessed homes, street-accessed homes (some with secondary dwelling units above the garages), and quaint cottages with detached secondary dwelling units facing a common green. At the lowest density, the community includes six-thousand-square-foot lots.

All of these elements combine to create a remarkable community that has garnered national press in the *New York Times*, *Wall Street Journal,* and *Builder* magazine. But the most remarkable thing about the community is that it is multigenerational by design. Every home at the Cannery is designed to Livable Design standards, making the homebuying decision democratic for all people, regardless of age or mobility.

Cut to opening day. After three years of hard work designing and planning the community, here it was: a tangible place we were walking through, along with throngs of people who came to experience for themselves the unique and beautiful characteristics of inclusive homes, meaningful open spaces, and urban trails connecting each piece to the rest and to the surrounding existing cultural infrastructure.

Everyone involved in the project upheld the goal of retaining an authenticity that honored the heritage of the site. The former Hunt-Wesson tomato canning operation now provides a community for a new generation of residents. It additionally demonstrates the art and science of farming, which is a legacy in this California community.

One of the tenets that we established for the community during the initial branding was the desire to allow adults to "re-experience the joy of living through a child's eyes." And watching people explore our vision brought to life was like being a little child on Christmas morning. Even seasoned building professionals expressed wide-eyed appreciation.

When I watched a toddler teetering across a zero-threshold by herself without dropping to a crawl and saw the look of pride on her father's face, my heart swelled with happiness. Later, I overheard a couple talking about how easy it was to move around in the home. I asked them how long they'd been married. "We're celebrating our golden anniversary this year!" replied the septuagenarian woman, beaming. I'll never forget how it felt to witness people representing both bookends of life enjoy the benefits of the same space.

Observing what we'd achieved, our team felt an incredible sense of camaraderie. One of the greatest joys of being an architect is to see people experience the spaces you have conceived and enjoy them!

People think they want a home that provides shelter, comfort, and convenience in a new, trouble-free, warranty-rich wrapper. But what we strive to deliver is far greater than that. We created a community that expands the typical demographic slice and combines all of these parts and pieces into a sanctuary. The whole being is greater than the sum of its parts.

A More Prosperous, Inclusive Future

Getting the Cannery designed, approved, and built was, for those at my firm and our partners, one of the greatest accomplishments in our recent body of work. But it was not easy.

The city of Davis is notoriously difficult to develop in, and the city government seems to like it that way. Our firm navigated multiple votes, approvals, and red-tape hurdles. Setting out, we knew the city's reputation—this project had failed to reach approval with two previous development teams—but our project team kept moving forward.

To the credit of the city of Davis, they know what they want. And one of the things they want is to be recognized as an innovation leader. Thus, one of the ways that the project team was able to satisfy that need was by providing a series of firsts: the first farm-to-fork community west of the Mississippi, the first "Dutch junction" (an intersection, common in the Netherlands, designed to protect bicyclists) in the US, and the first 100 percent Livable Design community in the country.

Livable Design was a tremendous inducement to the entitlement process. We were able to tell an authentic story about inclusivity, visitability, and multigenerational living, which touched the hearts of the community and its elected officials. The sales success of the community is a further testament to this vision, with the project nearing closeout just a few years after opening. This landmark community now stands as thriving proof that Livable Design, in concert with the Eight Elements of Community, allows residents to live happier, healthier, safer lives.

What I think the Cannery did so well is to show that you can't be one-dimensional about project design. I hear people in this industry talk about "green" all the time, and to that I ask, "Is that all you've got?" Green is great, but to me, that should be the baseline. We have a responsibility to be conscientious, and frankly, regulations are such that the building envelope is incredibly efficient in its own right. You can't just slap solar panels on a roof and expect buyers to come running.

So I ask again, "What else have you got?" We must be holistic in our concept, design, and execution, considering the Eight Elements of Community and Livable Design.

As I've said, I envision a future just five years from now in which one million Livable Design homes, townhomes, condominiums, and secondary dwelling units stand strong across this country—providing a sanctuary of warmth, comfort, beauty, and human dignity for every person who walks or wheels in the door. And they don't all have to be designed by my firm. (But they could be!)

They'll be designed and built by you and the valued colleagues you work with until Livable Design becomes a seamless part of how we live our lives. Until it becomes the expectation—the new normal.

It's easier than you may think to get started, because the push to incorporate Livable Design feels so *right*. Making a difference in the lives of people by simply doing what you do? That makes you feel like a rock star. Livable Design allows us to bring something of significance in what we design and build, while doing it attainably for builders and homebuyers alike.

You can be a brand ambassador for your organization, leveraging Livable Design to create a brand that authentically connects your firm to what your stakeholders really want and need out of a home. In the process, you can make your organization more profitable. You absolutely can (and should) do well *and* do good. Do not apologize for this! We are all in business to be successful and profitable.

The result will be a new housing industry, where today's problems are suddenly problems no longer: new homes without barriers for people of all ages and all mobility profiles. Imagine new model-home centers with no impediments to any of us being able to live a full life, with the respect, freedom, and dignity that every one of us deserves.

It takes courage to set yourself on a new path in any area of our life, and this step is no different. But with such remarkable rewards, Livable Design is worth every ounce of effort, and then some.

How to Get Started

When you are interested in getting involved in Livable Design, you don't have to do it alone. Whenever we embark on any new meaningful endeavor, it's beneficial to tap into the wisdom and experience of those who've done it before us.

Today, we have several thousand homes built, approved, and in the process of being built, all based on Livable Design. And we believe in this program so much that we've made it completely open source.

That's right. We're giving away the recipe for Coca-Cola, so to speak. Everything you need to start bringing your own Livable Design homes to life is available at www.livabledesign.com. We've made the program as simple to understand as following a recipe, with specific dimensions and clearances, areas to incorporate blocking, the type of hardware

Architecture
is hard
enough
when
everything
is
working

@gapingvoid

to use, and other design elements to consider if you want to go even further.

As an architect, a builder, or a developer, you need resources, and it's with you in mind that we created this program, so you can move forward down this path with commitment and confidence.

If you're looking for more of a full-service, hands-on experience from us, you can also engage us as consultants to either teach your organization the nuances of Livable Design or design an amazing new community for you. We can even work with you to create a branded program like we did with Bob Tummolo, Northern California Division President of Lennar in developing their Thoughtful Design℠ program. I'm also available for speaking engagements to share the benefits of Livable Design with people who haven't yet discovered its potential to revolutionize the way we design and build homes for the real people who live in them.

I'm committed to being your partner in bringing this dream to life—a million Livable Design homes across America over the next five years. It can be done. It will take many of us committed and working collaboratively towards that goal, and we can do it together.

The American Dream Reborn

In the short term, Livable Design can be the program that distinguishes you and your business from everyone else out there right now. And over the long term? You'll get to go to your lenders and say, "I'm the first builder in my market employing Livable Design. As a result, I'm outselling my competition by a ratio of two-to-one. You *want* to give me more money, because I've got a great story. And you need my story in your boardroom."

My wish for you is that you will look at this program and see the same incredible value that not only my team and clients, but also the thousands of people already living in these homes, have experienced. I want you to be as inspired as I am and to translate your inspiration into helping transform our industry to better serve those we're building for.

Our team has already done the immense amount of legwork required to create this program. We've paid the proverbial "dumb tax." All you need now is the courage to embrace it and make it your own. Once you do, and once others see your incredible work and the benefits to your business, they'll be lining up to join you.

Livable Design is a call to action for our entire industry. I'm thrilled to have answered the call. It has changed my life and my business and brought me a level of purpose, pride, success, and sense of accomplishment I never could have imagined.

I want this for you and your organization too—and for the people we're here to serve.

The next chapter of the American dream is only just beginning with Livable Design and its promise for a more attainable, beautiful, and adaptable future for all of us.

Will you answer that call?

The Future We Build

The most remarkable thing about Livable Design is that it is completely unremarkable.

With somewhere between 10 and 120 little elements, this unremarkable initiative takes common, off-the-shelf items and incorporates them in a new way. It demonstrates how these basic elements can change and enhance the lives of all people, from the life of a newborn to an octogenarian, and everyone in between.

My biggest fear in writing the story of Livable Design is that it seems so basic. Because this concept is so simple, it's easy to underestimate the depth of its impact.

Yet I've seen firsthand how Livable Design can profoundly change lives while simultaneously enhancing the significance you and your organization have in neighborhoods, loan committees, planning commissions, and the myriad of other stakeholders, agencies, and private and municipal entities that influence, mandate, and impact the homebuilding industry.

This is a phenomenon that will bring credibility and a human touch to an industry that is mostly underappreciated and misunderstood by individuals and institutions. Livable

Design is the higher purpose that the homebuilding industry has been missing for decades.

It is time for us to once again reinforce to the public why we do what we do—to provide this American dream—and why we do it with Livable Design. Because at the end of the day, if you're in this industry, it's because you love it and you love people. Additionally, you're an entrepreneur or part of an organization that operates and is led by someone with those values. Again, it is possible to do well *and* do good.

I know that this is change, and change is scary. It's hard. But here's the thing. If you don't like change, you're going to hate extinction!

Look, there are billions of dollars that circle the planet every day looking for a place to land. More often than not, they land with organizations that are principled, visionary, and value conscious—all within the framework of solid processes, procedures, and systems—and with teams whose members know the important part they play within those organizations.

When you add the purpose platform of Livable Design to your organization, you create a passionate and meaningful brand that is infectious to all the people you and your organization connect with. It's what I call the halo effect, and it comes from, as Peter Drucker said, "doing things right and doing the right things."

This aspect of business is the subject of a future book (stay tuned), but serves as a backdrop for the impact Livable Design can have when embraced by an organization of integrity, led by a passionate leader.

It doesn't take many ingredients to be remarkable, make an impact, enhance lives and living, and reach the highest level of success. Livable Design is a significant part of that vision.

Be remarkable. Take the first step.

"The journey of a thousand miles begins with a single step." – Lao Tzu

LIVABLE DESIGN

@gapingvoid

ABOUT THE AUTHOR

 Jeffrey DeMure, AIA, is working to breathe new life and promise into the American dream. A licensed architect with thirty-five plus years in the homebuilding industry, he is the founder of Jeffrey DeMure + Associates Architects Planners, Inc. Together with his team, DeMure has spent the last ten years developing Livable Design™, a revolutionary collection of simple, cost-effective elements that can be incorporated into the design of any living space to make it more fully inclusive for residents and guests of all ages and mobility profiles.

A nationally recognized speaker on topics ranging from architecture to entrepreneurialism, DeMure has addressed such notable forums as PCBC, ULI, NAHB's International Builders Show, The Seaside Institute, and many aging services associations nationally, including LeadingAge. He serves on numerous boards and advisory committees with the goal of sharing his vision for the future of the industry—a world where our homes and communities are built to grow with us over the course of an entire lifetime.

In addition to being a creative instigator, DeMure is a commercial pilot and loves a fine Moleskine notebook, a rOtring 600 pencil, and a space created with intent. He lives in Northern California with his wife, Melanie, and their four beautiful children, Emily, JT, Jeremy, and Brayden.

Are you ready to transform your business, the communities you touch, and the future of the building industry? Livable Design is the catalyst you need to bring purpose and passion back into your work. Jeff and his team offer:

- Speaking engagements—Bring Jeff to speak at your event, conference, or organization to share his vision of the building industry of tomorrow.

- Workshops—Learn from Jeff's team how to make the most of Livable Design and secure buy-in from colleagues, clients, and lenders.

- Free online resources—Access the entire list of Livable Design certified design elements at no cost.

- Design services—Hire Jeff and his team to create custom Livable Design plans for your project.

For more information, visit www.jdaarch.com or email Jeff and his team at livabledesign@jdaarch.com.